I0006414

Understanding, Hiring, and Using Managed Services Providers (MSPs) for Information Technology Outsourcing

Keith M. Cramer

outskirtspress

DENVER, COLORADO

Outskirts Press, Inc.
http://www.outskirtspress.com

ISBN: 978-1-4787-2741-5

Outskirts Press and the "OP" logo are trademarks belonging to Outskirts Press, Inc.

PRINTED IN THE UNITED STATES OF AMERICA

To my wife, Anjy. This handbook would not exist without her help, encouragement, and support.

Table of Contents

Credits, Acknowledgments, and Disclaimers

I want to thank my wife Anjy for encouraging me to work on this during a job hiatus. She also deserves credit for taking the author picture used on the back and for reading the manuscript and suggesting several modifications which make it easier to follow. It is fortuitous that we met in a writing class, and that she used to make her living writing grant proposals.

If you have any questions, comments, stories, or suggestions for future revisions, please e-mail me at **keithmcramer@gmail.com** and include the word "handbook" in the subject line. I am always looking for good examples to illustrate key points and any other ideas for improving this manual. If you share a story or a situation with me and I use it in a future edition, no personal or company identifiable information will be shared, though I need to have that information for verification and fact-checking purposes.

Finally, none of the examples contained herein should be understood to have occurred at any of the companies at which I've worked, though they might have, and any similarities to real-world situations are probably coincidental.

This work is obviously copyrighted by me, and any replication or use of it save for standard fair use (reviewing or sampling) is prohibited without my written consent. Not that I'm the Dickens of handbook writing, but I did make this. I also created the tables and graphics used inside. Any similarity to tables and graphics produced or created by anyone else is coincidental. I hold in high regard and respect all intellectual property, my own and that which was created by others. That being said, if you want to use something in this handbook, send me an e-mail and I will gladly consider your request, and likely we can work something out without having to re-write the Magna Carta.

Introduction:
Who I Am; What I Know

My career in information systems began in 1992, when MS-DOS was the operating system on most business PCs. Programs like Word, VisiCalc, and Lotus 1-2-3 were launched from menus; few people used Microsoft Windows. E-mail and the Internet were fairly new to the business world, and not everyone had access to them. Novell Netware was the consumer network operating system of choice, and Microsoft was still years away from releasing Active Directory.

Through the ensuing years, I have been a systems analyst, network administrator, acting director of Information Systems, vice president of Information Systems, and a consultant and senior engineer at a Washington, D.C.-based MSP. I went from using MSPs as a director and vice president, to working for one as a consultant.

My experience from both sides of the IT vendor relationship gives me a unique perspective on the challenges facing nontechnology companies and the computer companies which support them. I hope that you find the following pages engaging, informative, and insightful. I've tried to make it more than just a guide. I want this to be an instruction manual for a successful business partnership.

Enjoy the read.

Foreword: Why This Handbook?

Organized information is crucial in making decisions. The more you have, the better decisions you can make, and the fewer regrets you will have down the road. If I had known all of what I'm about to write at the beginning of my career, I would have made different, better decisions. This handbook is for both IT managers and nontechnical managers, though by necessity, I've written it for a nontechnical audience.

It is important to understand how we arrived at our present technical capability in order to understand the implications of the decisions we now make. This is to help frame one of the biggest problems facing all business enterprises: maintaining the right level of technology to best accomplish business goals in the most economical fashion possible.

Technological advances tend to compound over time. Each achievement spawns myriad others. Accounting developed along with written language more than 7,000 years ago, and was accomplished on, among other media, clay tablets. Transactions could take months or years to complete. It took over 6,500 years for someone to come up with the idea for double-entry bookkeeping (first described in the fifteenth century during the Western Renaissance), and then another 400 years for the invention of the first programmable computer. The

Internet was first tested successfully on October 29, 1969, and first crashed after the third letter was typed during that same test. Robert Metcalf at Xerox invented Ethernet Networking in 1973, and on April 1, 1976, Steve Jobs and Steve Wozniak released the Apple I, the first commercial personal computer. VisiCalc, the first spreadsheet program, was born in 1979 on the Apple II, and a new era of accounting was born. In an internal paper at Compaq Computer Corporation in 1996, the word "cloud" was first used to describe the Internet.

Through the 1990s and 2000s, companies leveraged information technology to facilitate productivity, and not just with accounting applications (though for the first 20 years of the information age, the IT department reported to the head of accounting, typically the CFO). During that time, as companies built their internal computer networks, the amount of data grew, and the complexity of these systems increased exponentially. But still, technology was fairly predictable and easy to manage. The servers were in a closet or a dedicated LAN room with separate power and air conditioning. If there was a problem, a computer technician went into the LAN room and fixed it.

Today, most accounting is done on commercial computer systems or full-scale ERP (Enterprise Resource Planning) systems, and Ethernet connects most computers to the Internet. Information systems are all-encompassing, including accounting, correspondence, reporting, information exchange, inventory control, telecommunications, security and encryption, cross-platform translation, databases, e-mail, voice mail, marketing, and the integration of all of the above. Every public company has a Web site, and most private companies do as well. It is possible to do business exclusively on the Internet (e.g., you can shop for, purchase, and view or listen to songs, movies, or books instantly on the same device). The newly minted CIO has been added to the corporate pantheon of officers and reports directly to the CEO.

It is not only possible to forgo the LAN room or the computer closet, in many cases it makes perfect business sense to do so. New companies no longer must invest in servers and software and the personnel to configure them because these are offered by vendors as services. Companies who currently have a significant investment in hardware can opt to replace their systems as needed with Internet-based services in the cloud. No longer are your business processes or data at the mercy of your building's infrastructure, your dedicated power and air-conditioning, the electric grid, or local crises such as storms, floods, traffic, street closures, strikes, fires, police actions, bomb scares, or accidents. And even more attractive: if and when you move your offices, you will have very little, if any, downtime.

Some hardware must remain on-site, like terminals, Internet connections, firewalls, print servers and printer/copiers, but for the most part, companies now have the choice to subscribe to everything on cloud-based systems, or to move their entire infrastructure to the cloud.

To get to the cloud, businesses will need to partner with one or multiple technology companies. Requirements analyses, current network assessments, project management, and industry knowledge are all key to finding the perfect solution for your company. The right partner for your business could be an MSP, or managed services provider.

If your company is not interested in moving to the cloud, the MSP can support your network and computer infrastructure and advise you of current technology trends. Next to full-time IT staff, the MSP is the best way to manage your IT infrastructure.

This handbook describes what MSPs do, what it means to engage and use an MSP (how to create an RFP to which MSPs will respond with viable proposals), and will familiarize you with some of the lingo used by MSPs to describe their services. A glossary of terms used within the information technology industry is included at the end. Many IT acronyms share meanings with acronyms in other industries, and searching the Internet for the right definition can cause confusion if you don't already know a little about what you are looking for. Finally, this handbook will describe how to successfully work with an MSP.

There are literally hundreds of thousands of information technology choices companies must make to be productive and remain competitive. From different virtual infrastructures (VMWare ESXi, Microsoft's Hyper-V and APP-V, Citrix, Amazon's AWS, and VMWare's vCloud), to document management solutions and cost recovery solutions, to centralized management of mobile devices, to remote access, to office productivity software, to backup and disaster avoidance and recovery solutions, the options are nearly limitless. There are as many disaster avoidance and recovery schemes as there are CIOs. And cloud computing is on every network diagram or wish list.

The ability to sort through the IT marketplace and make good choices for your business is, now, the best skill to have. A successful MSP engagement can help you make sense of all these trends and guide your company to a technology strategy which is viable for years to come. An unsuccessful engagement will be a costly waste of time and money. The best way to hire the MSP which is right for your company is to pay attention, do your due diligence, and have crystal clear expectations. Reading this handbook is an excellent beginning.

1

What Is a Managed Services Provider (MSP)?

Distilled into the most general language, MSPs are vendors which provide a company a managed service like IT management, payroll processing, HR, or accounting services. Companies need to keep costs down and invest in their core business; money and resources not dedicated to the core business are a burden. If you are a construction company, it usually makes more sense to invest your capital in a bulldozer than in an accounting application, a payroll clerk, or an e-mail system.

As far as this handbook is concerned, *an MSP is a technology company which sells its expertise and processes as services to non-technology companies on a contractual engagement and provides service level agreements (SLAs) to their clients.* The services being sold by the MSP are technology services: computer expertise, technology help, consulting, etc. The other way to say it is that *the MSP is your IT department.* If you already have an IT department, the MSP can act in concert with your staff to fill advisory or operational gaps that might exist in your organization. In this case, the MSP is a value-added reseller (VAR) of IT services to augment existing staff capabilities. This is more common as IT service offerings compound in quality and quantity on an almost daily basis.

There are many MSPs in the market. Like the myriad smartphones and tablets available today, these companies are similar in many ways, yet in other ways, are completely different. Some MSPs work only in dedicated vertical markets (health care, legal, finance, nonprofit, government). Some are generalists and will take on and assist any type of client.

MSPs offer a wide range of services, from computer support, to strategic and operational consulting, to project management, to the remote management and monitoring (RMM) of your network, to systems analysis and engineering, to a help desk function for your organization. Many also act as a value-added reseller (VAR) for software and hardware, making it easy to get new services and products ordered, delivered, and installed quickly. Using an MSP is like having your own fully staffed IT department at a fraction of the cost you would spend on personnel of your own.

Many MSPs offer customizable, à la carte solutions. You can hire multiple MSPs to handle different aspects of your information systems: you might choose one MSP as a strategic IT advisor and choose another one to handle the operational side of your information technology systems. This might be a good solution for a company preparing to grow or change. This is a perfectly normal arrangement, though it can get ugly if roles are not strictly delineated.

If your business is in a specialized vertical market, like law, health care, finance, or is nonprofit, not all MSPs will service your line of business or are qualified to do so. For example, many law firms use document management systems, and many health-care providers use medical billing and inventory control software and have HIPAA (and HITECH) compliance requirements. Financial institutions are subject to FINRA compliance regulations, and companies which process credit card information are subject to PCI-DSS regulations. Not all MSPs have expertise in supporting these systems, but there are usually specialty MSPs working in your market. Keep this in mind when issuing your RFP and when evaluating the proposals.

There are possible downsides to using an MSP. The lack of a constant technical support presence in your office can be frustrating, especially for demanding personnel or companies over 40 people in size. Security concerns can be a big issue as well: some regulatory requirements demand more robust security procedures, and you will have to trust an MSP to a great degree (if a system admin can steal data from the NSA and fly to Hong Kong, a person in a similar position at an MSP with similar access to your data can choose to be indiscreet with it as well). There may be uses for technology that are not recognized or utilized because a technology person is just not there to witness day-to-day operations. Finally, an inadequate level of communication between your company and the MSP can lead to prioritization missteps and service dissatisfaction.

Managing the MSP is an important job function and should not be thought of as an incidental responsibility. A substantial, continual investment of your time and resources is required in order to maintain a positive relationship with the MSP and good results for your company. The MSP is not like the break-fix vendor for your printers, copiers, or postage machines. The MSP is fully integrated in your daily operations; this is a very intimate relationship. In sales presentations, MSPs acknowledge this intimacy by redefining the customer/vendor relationship between your two companies as a "partnership."

2

MSP Services—Getting Specific

The break-fix computer support vendor is the basic level of computer support: The person or company you call to fix computer problems on a time and materials (T&M) basis. They bill you an hourly rate, plus any parts or software they need to buy. The MSP is the next level in the computer support hierarchy.

An MSP is paid a monthly fee to provide a set of IT services under a service level agreement (SLA) and to be responsible for addressing any IT problems at your company.

MSPs typically have a lot of talent in their organization. Perhaps as a result of this, many will offer additional services over and above standard managed services. This is where MSPs begin to cross over into the areas of IT and management consulting.

Here are some of the different types of services offered by MSPs and where they fall in a simple classification matrix between operations, advisory, and Internet-based operations:

Managed Services (Operations and Support Services)	CIO Services (Advisory and Strategic Consulting)	Hosted Services (Internet-Based Solutions/Operations)
Hardware and Software Repair and Maintenance (Break-Fix)	Interim IT Management	E-Mail Outsourcing (Hosted E-Mail)
Remote Management and Monitoring (RMM)	IT Staffing	Public Cloud-Based Networking (Hosted Servers/Desktops)
Help Desk	Organizational Review and Restructuring	Virtualized Services & Infrastructure CMS
Private Cloud (Virtualized Servers/Desktops)	IT Strategy/Multiyear Planning	SharePoint Hosting
Hardware and Software Upgrades	Policies and Procedures Development	Off-Site Backup and Synch
Project Management	IT Auditing (Third-Party IT Review)	E-Mail Spam and Virus Cleaning
Network Design and Implementation	Disaster Avoidance and Recovery Planning	E-Mail Archiving
Network Security (Network Admin, Antivirus, Firewall, etc.)	Project Management	Hybrid Networks (Combination of On-Site and Hosted Services)
System Upgrades and Reengineering	Vendor Review and Selection	
Site Visits/Wellness Visits	Vendor Management	

Managed Services
(Operations and Support Services)

Managed services are typically operational/transactional. If you are a small company contemplating whether to replace your current T&M/Break-Fix computer vendor with an MSP, many of these are services you are probably already using with your existing company, with a couple of exceptions.

1. Hardware and Software Repair and Maintenance (Break-Fix)

All MSPs offer hardware and software repair and maintenance. It is the most basic service in the computer support industry, and even MSPs who have relatively few service offerings will provide it. Chances are your company has employed a break-fix/time and materials vendor in the past. Unless otherwise noted, MSPs do not charge separately for fixing computers and updating software unless it is obvious that the cause was employee negligence (got a virus, spilled a drink, etc.).

When a computer breaks, they will work with your employees to fix it via the phone or remote control. If that does not work, they will send someone to your location to further explore the issue and attempt to resolve it.

Software manufacturers offer regular security and functional updates. Microsoft and Apple are two companies which release updates to their software regularly, and in order to keep your systems running at peak functionality and with the latest updates to thwart malicious software, their software should be regularly updated and maintained. The MSP will have an update plan or scheme for your systems. It is usually best to keep your computers and servers up to date.

2. Remote Management and Monitoring (RMM)

This is the entry-level service offering of MSPs and is what distinguishes them from break-fix-only vendors; it is the "meat" of managed services. There are several ways to monitor and manage computer systems remotely, and MSPs typically utilize multiple methods. One way is by installing applications, called "agents," on your computers, servers, and network which monitor all aspects of system health and report back to the MSP data-collection point. By collecting this information and processing it at a central location, the MSP can monitor your system 24/7/365.

RMM agents never sleep unless the systems on which they reside are turned off. If an agent detects a problem, it triggers an alarm which can alert the MSP. Depending on the service level agreement (SLA), the MSP will take certain predefined actions to address the problem. For example, assume that your Internet connection goes down at 1:00 A.M. The illustration shows the advantage between using an MSP and relying on yourself.

RMM vs. Non-RMM Problem Response

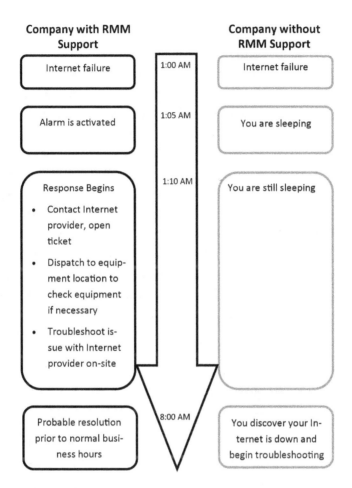

Company with RMM Support | Company without RMM Support

	Time	
Internet failure	1:00 AM	Internet failure
Alarm is activated	1:05 AM	You are sleeping
Response Begins • Contact Internet provider, open ticket • Dispatch to equipment location to check equipment if necessary • Troubleshoot issue with Internet provider on-site	1:10 AM	You are still sleeping
Probable resolution prior to normal business hours	8:00 AM	You discover your Internet is down and begin troubleshooting

3. Help Desk

   If RMM is the "meat" of the MSP world, then the help desk is the "potatoes." This is the second traditional staple of the MSP. They will have a help desk staffed with personnel who answer phone calls, create and track trouble tickets, and help your employees with routine computer and technology problems throughout the day. These kinds of problems can be anything from how to set up a smartphone to get their corporate e-mail, to fixing printing issues, to helping in the recovery of a computer from a virus.

4. Private Cloud (Customer Equipment/Virtualized Servers/Desktops)

    The cloud is widely understood to be the public Internet infrastructure, using shared resources. It is also possible to maintain what is known as a private cloud, by which a customer's infrastructure or equipment is not shared by other entities. One example of this would be a company which recently upgraded the hardware and software for their Exchange server. The company then decided they would best be served from a disaster avoidance and recovery standpoint by putting their e-mail in the cloud. So as to not lose their investment in new hardware and software, they hired a company to put their server in a rack at the data warehouse and maintain it there. They get Internet and power redundancy and a climate-controlled room for their server, and only they use it. Another commonly accepted example would be a company virtualizing their servers and/or desktops on their own premises, though this is more appropriately termed "cloud emulation" since no public infrastructure is utilized.

5. Hardware and Software Upgrades

    This is different from hardware and software maintenance. New computers and software frequently need to be purchased, installed, and configured, and this is something MSPs do regularly.

6. Project Management

    This is listed under both CIO/advisory services and managed services. IT projects undertaken by your MSP will have an internal project manager to coordinate the communication, allocate and schedule resources, and monitor the progress of the activity. The CIO/advisor function also performs project management, but these are typically complex activities which are cross-organizational in nature, usually involving the MSP, customer employees, and other customer vendors.

7. Network Design and Implementation

If the MSP is going to support your existing network, they should have the capability to create a new one for you if required. The MSP can design, build, test, and deploy a network. This can include features of public or private cloud, or encompass them exclusively. It can also be in addition to an existing network; for example, if a client decides to begin sharing their space with another company, and the other company needs to be on a separate network segment.

8. Network Security (Network Admin, Antivirus, Firewall)

The MSP will do a network security assessment which will show who has access to what, and what is exposed. This can encompass the network itself, Internet access (and access to the private network from the Internet), server security, and file security. It also includes antivirus, as many viruses can steal data and passwords. It is fairly common for companies who have managed their own network to have granted full access to all files to everyone, or to have no corporate antivirus program or policies. All these issues have ramifications which are rarely fully understood by the company until it is too late.

9. System Upgrades and Reengineering

Sometimes a company needs to implement new technology to stay competitive in their core business. This could be anything from installing a new accounting system or document management system, to rolling out a new computer operating system and office productivity package to the entire company at once. This is a major project, and most MSPs should have the talent to get this done.

10. Site Visits (Wellness Visits)

Most MSP contracts call for minimal on-site time, usually once a month. It is simply cheaper and more efficient for the MSP to be able to support clients remotely, either by phone or by remote-support software. Site visits are a good way for an MSP technician to evaluate the state of the IT systems in the client office and are a good opportunity to interact with company employees.

Despite having telephone and e-mail access to MSP personnel, many employees do not think to engage the MSP unless there is someone from the MSP on-site. I have been on the phone with my client contacts prior to making a site visit to check to see if there were any issues that I needed to prepare to address. The clients typically report that there are no active issues, but when I arrive, almost everyone has at least one question, and several people usually have issues which take significant time to address. Many MSPs will allow, by default, a certain number of hours for a technician to visit your office. A minimal monthly visit should be built into most contracts. After all, there is no substitute for having experienced eyes and hands attending to your infrastructure and dealing directly with your people.

If you want more visits than the contract allows, ask. It may cost more money, but having a resource at your office can go a long way to keeping your internal customers happy. I have heard some MSPs are moving away from this business model, but there is, again, no substitute for having a personalized visit. Bad battery indicator lights, server status lights, and more can be easily seen by a trained technician, which won't necessarily be part of what the MSP is monitoring, or can monitor, remotely.

CIO Services (Advisory and Strategic Consulting)

CIO services are typically strategic or advisory in nature. If you are a small company contemplating whether to replace your current T&M/break-fix computer vendor with an MSP, it is very unlikely that your current vendor provides these services. This is a big reason why many companies choose to "upgrade" to an MSP from a break-fix/ T&M vendor.

1. Interim IT Management

Sometimes an organization needs temporary help. Either the person or persons responsible for IT has left or the company finds itself in uncharted technical territory. Perhaps the existing IT staff has become too difficult to manage. It makes sense to have someone who understands the operational and strategic sides of IT take control and manage it for the rest of the non-technical stakeholders.

2. IT Staffing

Organizations frequently need assistance in hiring technical staff. Headhunters and HR departments can help, but if there is no one capable of evaluating the technical qualifications and curricula vitae of potential hires, they won't get you from here to there.

3. Organizational Review and Restructuring

A CIO-level advisor can evaluate the technology needs of a company and translate these into position descriptions, which can then be used to reclassify/retrain existing IT staff or hire new personnel. This can sometimes be as simple as getting the right people currently on staff into the appropriate job track. Occasionally, this might mean existing staff must go. This type of review should be handled gingerly: it is no surprise that most IT people have seen "consultants" come in to an organization and run roughshod over the existing systems and personnel in place. Typically, as soon as existing personnel become aware this is being done, they have their résumés out the door. Don't lose key personnel to bad communication. Also, as a customer, you may want to take with a grain of salt any recommendations arising from this kind of organizational review. Major changes could be recommended in order to justify the review. There are many ways to achieve any operational or strategic goal, and just because a consultant recommends a different path does not mean your current path will not get you to the same destination.

4. IT Strategy/Multiyear Planning

Technology is changing the way businesses function, and the trend has been for more comprehensive, specialized, and cheaper technology options. The trend has increased almost exponentially since cloud services first appeared, and it is important to stay abreast of the latest developments. MSPs are steeped in the technology field and can help to spot trends and guide your business decisions into the future.

5. Policies and Procedures Development

Documentation is an important part of managing and controlling information systems. From a legal perspective, if an employee commits a crime using a computer or system at your company, you may be liable. Formulating a computer-use policy which employees must read and accept can mitigate company liability. It also shows them what is and is not appropriate use of company resources. Computer and network procedures are necessary to keep track of the steps to create computer accounts, share documents, set up firewall rules, set up personal computers and smartphones, and everything else you can think of which requires proper authorization and steps to accomplish IT tasks.

6. IT Auditing (Third-Party IT Review)

It is always a good idea to get a second opinion in major medical matters, and this also applies to your information technology position. Whether it is to confirm your current operational level regarding all things IT or if it is being done because you don't know your existing systems any longer, for whatever reason, you should have an IT audit. I recommend a good audit at least once per year, preferably before budget season. If you have a current IT provider, it is a good idea to get an audit accomplished by another provider every few years. Most MSPs will do an IT review at least once per year, but there is no substitute for an independent audit.

7. Disaster Avoidance and Recovery Planning

Many companies' disaster avoidance and recovery planning consists of making sure they have off-site backups of their data and uninterruptible e-mail in the case of an emergency. This is well and good, but is the bare minimum of a disaster avoidance and recovery plan. What most companies fail to factor in is the process involved in weathering a disaster or crisis, the time it will take to get back to good, and the interim steps necessary for the business to continue to function. How, for example, would a company run their accounts receivable and accounts payable if they could not access the office to do their books? How long will their vendors go without being paid? What are the ramifications of unanswered business telephone calls? How will employees be able to access the data that has been backed up remotely? How about e-mail?

There is an entire body of certifications for the profession of disaster avoidance and recovery planning project management, and more than 95 percent of companies believe what they currently have is okay. This is false confidence.

However, I would also caution against throwing resources at the issue until you have assessed your risk and your current position.

8. Vendor Review and Selection

Almost every service vendor impacts IT decisions. Copiers, printers, scanners, postage machines, fax machines, telephone systems, videoconferencing, and AV equipment: all of these can, and do, cross over into the IT arena. I have many stories about vendors being engaged without the proper notification of the IT department and processes which had to be restarted because certain requirements weren't met. Additionally, vendors who sell IT goods and services, like Web sites, SEO, and database development, all fall under the auspices of IT, and it would do well to have an IT consultant who has your back involved in these conversations, if only in an advisory capacity.

9. Vendor Management

Many companies have multiple vendors (see above) which, at times, need careful scheduling and planning in order to operate properly together.

Hosted Services (Internet-Based Solutions)

Hosted solutions have been emerging over the past few years. Many MSPs are now offering to "host" your servers or services in a secure, off-site, "colocation" facility, or data center. These data centers are called colocation facilities because they act as another physical location for your company's infrastructure. The hosted solutions can range in scope from relocating your physical servers to a data center, to taking specific services from your network, like e-mail, file storage, security and authentication, backup, and even desktop replication, to the data center. Sometimes the MSP will control the data-center hardware and environment, and sometimes the MSP will resell hosting services from another provider, like Amazon (AWS) or Rackspace. The prerequisite for this type of solution implementation to work properly is fast Internet connectivity from your business location(s) to the data center.

Almost any application can be hosted, provided there is enough Internet bandwidth and low latency between your office and the colocation facility. This can be a very attractive alternative to having your hardware at your business location and fits nicely with disaster avoidance and recovery planning (DARP).

1. E-Mail Outsourcing (Hosted E-Mail)

This is probably the most common service to be outsourced, and there are a lot of choices. The two largest computer companies in America, Google and Microsoft (Google Apps and Microsoft Office 365, respectively), both offer hosted e-mail services. There are numerous vendors who also sell other hosted e-mail solutions and also hosted Exchange solutions (if you want to stick with Exchange but don't want to have to manage your own server). Depending on your requirements, these services can cost anywhere from "free" to about $15 per account. Some MSPs will offer to host your e-mail on their equipment or at their data center as part of their subscription package.

2. Public Cloud-Based Networking (Hosted Servers/Desktops)

    In this scenario, one or more of your servers are in the cloud, on equipment that also runs servers for other people. Usually this is a virtualized infrastructure, and there is no chance your servers or data will be seen by any other company. Hosted desktops are fairly new: VMware's VDI, Microsoft's Hyper-V, and Citrix's XenDesktop are all commercially available VDI offerings and can run at a data center. You can attach to your desktop from work, home, or when you're on the road, and the desktop will be the same no matter where you are. All desktop and server data is kept in the data center, so if your work, home, or mobile computer stops working or is stolen, your desktop and data are safe. Just turn on a new computer, point it at your remote desktop, and begin where you left off (even if you were in mid-edit of a document). MSPs are in this arena, and it is poised to grow tremendously over the next few years. It is a high-availability (HA) technology and is great for disaster and recovery planning, making it a strong, secure choice for organizations.

3. Virtualized Services & Infrastructure CMS

    Some services can be hosted in the cloud, like document management, accounting, payroll, enterprise resources management (ERM), customer resource management (CRM) systems like SalesForce.com, etc. Most companies already utilize this feature and don't realize it: their corporate Web site is a service hosted by a third party, usually utilizing another party's Web-server.

4. SharePoint Hosting

   SharePoint and other secure intellectual property sharing and collaboration services are available inexpensively on the Web. The only real cost to getting this up and running is labor for development of a site and administrative setup. This can be fairly inexpensive, and it's much cheaper to deploy than a SharePoint site built and managed internally.

5. Off-Site Backup and Synch

   This is a common hosted service today. In fact, most people utilize it at home in the form of Apple's iCloud, Microsoft's OneDrive (formerly SkyDrive), Google Drive, or Box. Sophisticated backup schemes can back up your entire infrastructure, including your running servers, to the cloud and can have your servers completely restored in the cloud immediately if you have a disaster, and these services can also have a live server shipped to you within hours of a catastrophe. Of course, you have to pay a considerable amount to achieve this level of disaster recovery, but it can be worth it.

6. Spam Cleaning

   Before e-mail hits your mail server, hosted or otherwise, it can be directed through a sophisticated spam filter which scans and classifies e-mail through automated processes. This is almost a requirement in today's information age.

7. E-Mail Archiving

   Commercial e-mail systems have been around for over 20 years, and there are people who like to keep all of their e-mails. There are legal and regulatory reasons which require companies to keep e-mail far beyond their useful life, and because of these reasons, e-mail archiving is frequently necessary. Hosted e-mail archiving keeps your corporate e-mail out of your mail server, saving you space and allowing you to access it from anywhere should you need to.

8. Hybrid Networks (Combination of On-Site and Hosted Services)

Hybrid systems describe your network state if it consists of both on-site and cloud-based software and services. For example, it has become popular over the past few years for smaller companies to outsource their e-mail, rather than spend a great deal of money to run an e-mail server on premises; likewise with SharePoint services. A huge benefit to this is not only that your company can save the money for upgrading the servers every 4 or 5 years, but also that the hosted systems are not dependent upon your office Internet connection, which has several critical weaknesses.

To understand the difference between *hybrid networks* and other kinds of networks, see the figures on the following pages. The *traditional network* is characterized by having all of the technology, systems, and software in one physical location. The *hybrid network* is characterized by having mission-critical technology and systems in the customer's physical location and at a data center, and a fully *cloud-based network* is characterized by having all mission-critical technology and systems at the data center, i.e. "in the cloud."

Traditional Network

The Internet (Cloud)

Your Company Office

Your On-Premises Network

-Firewall
-File-sharing servers
-E-mail servers
-Application servers
-Print/Scan servers
-Network backup

Hybrid Network

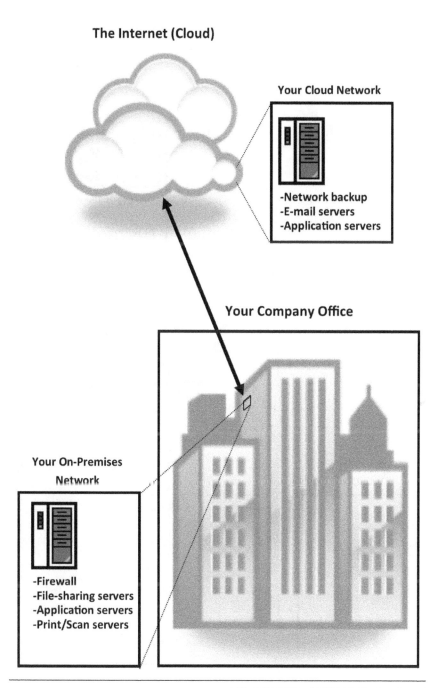

The Internet (Cloud)

Your Cloud Network

-Network backup
-E-mail servers
-Application servers

Your Company Office

Your On-Premises
Network

-Firewall
-File-sharing servers
-Application servers
-Print/Scan servers

Cloud-Based Network

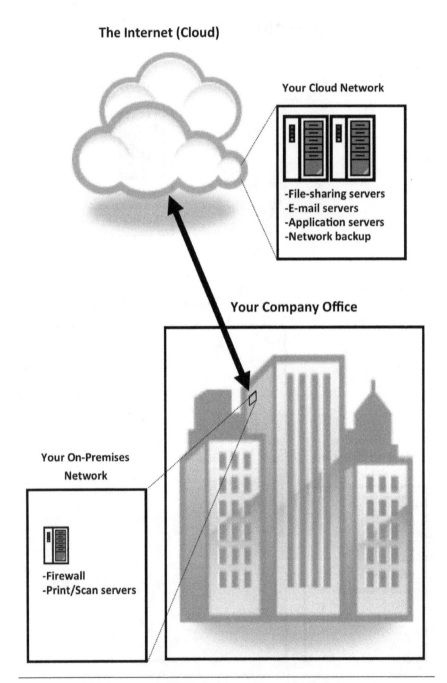

The Internet (Cloud)

Your Cloud Network

-File-sharing servers
-E-mail servers
-Application servers
-Network backup

Your Company Office

Your On-Premises
Network

-Firewall
-Print/Scan servers

3

Why Choose an MSP?

Inexpensive, Well-Rounded IT Service

Most small businesses have one or two servers in a coat closet, an Internet connection, a firewall, and some computers. Someone in the office can restart the server when there is a problem, but not all problems can be solved this way (nor should they be). It is best to have an expert who works with servers, networks, and computers handle the inevitable problems that will come up with this equipment. The data on the servers and the computers are critical for the survivability of the business, and trusting this to a nonexpert is not a prudent business decision. A trained and experienced IT professional should handle your critical IT infrastructure.

Unfortunately, most small businesses cannot afford to hire a full-time IT professional, which can cost anywhere from $60,000 upward per year, depending on the geographic area. Likewise, most IT professionals have specialties, and an IT engineer or system admin might not be the right person to help employees with general computer issues. Your IT person might be great at maintaining a network, but may not be very good at adding to it as needed. Sometimes a small business can get lucky and hire a computer person who can fill multiple roles, but there is no guarantee of a good fit. As far as certifications go, they do not guarantee practical skills, troubleshooting skills, communication skills, or critical thinking capabilities.

MSPs have the advantage of being able to hire multiple technology specialists, more than a small business could ever afford. MSPs have CIO equivalent consultants able to advise you of IT strategy and operations; project managers; e-mail, and internal security specialists; firewall, VPN, and networking specialists; as well as help desk staff. Properly deployed, this phalanx of skilled technology workers will beat any in-house IT staff for exposure, breadth of experience, education, and flexibility.

MSPs do not take vacations. One of the advantages of using an MSP is that in emergencies, indispensable skills are never out of reach, even if individuals are.

Finally, most MSPs bundle their services, so you will get more than just help desk services or remote management and monitoring (RMM) of your network equipment: antivirus software, e-mail spam filtering, hosted Exchange e-mail, server hosting, and cloud-based computing are examples of some of the "free" services MSPs can and will offer if you sign on the bottom line.

MSPs will monitor your equipment for problems. The agents they install on your computers and servers will report a problem, usually before anyone in your organization is aware of it.

Augmentation of IT Staff

Some small businesses, and many midsize businesses, have the resources to maintain an internal IT staff. Internal IT is good for dealing immediately with people and problems inside the company, installing programs, cleaning viruses, and dealing with occasional infrastructure issues. It is also good to have staff on board who owe their primary loyalty to their company, without any possibility of split-company priorities. However, internal IT staff will need help from time to time, and MSPs can fill this role. Some MSPs will allow internal IT staff to have access to their support portal so they can use the same RMM (remote monitoring and management) tools as the MSP technicians. And, as mentioned before, MSPs do not take vacations, so when your IT staff is away, the MSP can be a handy backup.

Replacement of IT Staff

Sometimes a company will find it necessary to replace their existing IT staff. Decisions like this are never made lightly or quickly. An MSP could be a good way to fill the IT role. An MSP will most certainly be more cost-effective than hiring an IT employee or employees. Usually there are multiple technical specialties involved in deploying or operating a network, and it is unlikely that any one IT person straddles all of those proficiencies. An MSP will have IT personnel who are experts in the various technologies comprising your network.

The downside to replacing IT staff with an MSP is that there won't be anyone from IT at your office, and this is a sacrifice many companies are not willing or are unable to make. It is one thing to have to wait for help from someone in your organization's IT department; it is quite another thing to have to call a third party, speak with someone who will only take your information and start a trouble ticket, and then have to wait for an appropriate resource to call you back, which could take anywhere from between 15 minutes to the next day. This person may or may not be able to fix your problem, and it may need to be escalated to someone else, which is a further delay. When you pick up the phone, you may as well be calling someone in Timbuktu as down the street for all the satisfaction it will bring.

Companies who have a "high-touch" need will either need to change their expectations or hire an MSP who, at an additional cost, will dedicate more resources to the organization or place someone at their location permanently. This model is becoming more and more popular as companies demand faster response times and a personal touch to their help desk solution.

4

The MSP's Responsibilities

Your chosen MSP will be responsible for whatever your contract states, but some "typical" responsibilities include your network operations, the maintenance and well-being of computers and hardware attached to your network, your firewall, and your Internet connection. But the exact nature of the MSP's responsibilities and the speed with which they are obligated to respond to problems will be closely tied to the price you pay for the service and depend largely on your service level agreement (SLA) with the MSP.

Technology Monitoring, Management, and Intervention

The MSP is typically tasked with remote management and monitoring (RMM) of your critical equipment and will act on alerts according to the SLA in your contract. This includes a comprehensive action or decision tree, so that during emergencies, you and the MSP thoroughly understand your roles, responsibilities, and expectations.

Reporting (Tickets, Utilization Stats)

The MSP is tasked with tracking tickets and monitoring data having to do with your network and network operations. Solid reporting is required to be able to pinpoint issues before they become chronic or malignant, and the MSP should be able to give you monthly or quarterly summary reports (i.e., executive summaries) on activities for your network. This is also how the MSP justifies their existence; look to reports to brag about proactive actions taken and problems solved.

It is also good to be able to spot trends in order to better plan what you will need to do in the future. This is part of what is called strategic planning. For example, if you see a report that shows your Internet activity is starting to grow and take up your company's available bandwidth, you can instruct the MSP to investigate that and make plans to get more bandwidth, if needed. If you see that a particular drive on your file server is filling up, you can plan ahead so that you don't run out of space. It is never a good idea to remedy a problem with a temporary or stopgap solution; true solutions can take many months to roll out.

Advising (CIO Services)

One of the big advantages to having an MSP, besides their operational role, is their strategic or advisory role. Your MSP account manager will keep in touch with you regularly and keep abreast of the direction and health of your company. There will be a strategic person at the MSP which the account manager talks to about your company and its direction, and this is so there are no "Aha! Gotcha!" surprises. This advisor will help you spot trends (good and bad) and prepare you to respond to them with a plan.

Good reporting and good communication are crucial to strategic planning. Ideally, your MSP reviews your monthly or quarterly reports with a strategic eye and schedules a meeting with you to discuss it. During this meeting you might discuss any issues or concerns you may have that aren't shown in the reports (someone is using the Internet to stream movies, which reduces the available bandwidth for other employees' legitimate Internet usage) or bring up new issues. If you are preparing to replace your copiers, move, hire, or lay off personnel in the upcoming months, it is imperative to alert the MSP as soon as you know so the MSP can properly advise you and plan their resources to be available to make the process as smooth as possible.

Sometimes company officers are reluctant to disclose too much to the MSP for fear of incurring additional charges. Sometimes it seems as if the MSP wants to do nothing but create new projects so they can charge you extra. While this is true, it is not nefarious behavior. MSPs would like any changes to your network infrastructure to be a project, so that it benefits from the rigors of a project plan and life cycle. With a project, more people are involved, more oversight is applied to the task, and more potential problems can be avoided. This stems from an abundance of caution based on real-world experience, and your company will do well to follow their recommendations. As Benjamin Franklin once said, "An ounce of prevention is worth a pound of cure."

MSP Employees

The Account Manager (or Salesperson)

The account manager may be the person who answered your RFP, came to your office, and won your business. He or she is your primary contact at the MSP and is not necessarily someone who is technically proficient.

The account manager will meet with you regularly to discuss your operational and strategic goals, get your input on the quality of service you are receiving, and present solutions to you in the form of purchase orders, statements of work (SOWs), or project proposals. If you have a problem with an invoice, you will talk to your account manager. If you or one of your employees are moved to report an especially exceptional occurrence with an employee of the MSP, you would tell it to your account manager. If you want to switch from a tape backup system to a more robust online system, you would express this to your account manager. The account manager can schedule technicians, follow up on projects, and be your advocate inside the MSP. The account manager is not usually the strategic advisor at the MSP, but is rather the conduit of the strategic advisor, or the facilitator of the meeting.

The Engineers

Engineers (and, to a lesser degree, help desk personnel) are charged with keeping your network physically up and running and ensuring your business has uninterrupted continual use of and access to network resources like e-mail, files, printers, copiers, scanners, and the Internet. As a customer, you will have contact with the pros only when they are working on a problem directly involving you (i.e., a ticketed problem). Engineers are not necessarily the best at communicating complex technical issues to nontechnical people on the fly, while responding to an emergency or problem. (So if they are in your office, working on an emergency, it is still best for you to contact your account manager for status updates.)

The Help Desk Technicians

Different MSPs structure their help desk services in different ways. Sometimes the initial call to the help desk will only result in a ticket being created and given to the caller, with very little, if any, troubleshooting occurring at this time. Typically, this level of specialization is used in larger help desk environments. Regardless, this initial call is followed by a call from a help desk technician, usually within the time frame of the service level agreement (SLA). This technician will gather more information and begin troubleshooting the problem with the ticket holder.

The Project Manager

This person is typically the overarching coordinator of technical resources, purchasing, and communication with you and other stakeholders at your company about ongoing projects. Sometimes, but not always, this is your account manager. Typical projects such as a hardware/software refresh of desktops and servers can last 6–9 months and can require daily contact between the project manager and a point of contact at your company (probably you).

The Advisor (or, the CIO)

The advisor is your chief information officer. This is widely defined as being a strategic or visionary position, but in smaller companies, the CIO is involved in operations as well. The CIO will advise you on technology matters ranging from operational best practices to your company's long-term IT strategy.

5

Managing the MSP—
Your Responsibilities

The MSP will act as your IT department, so you will need to treat them as such. They will require some level of interactive management. Depending on the size of your company and the level of engagement of your MSP, you should spend between 5–15 percent of your time dealing with them, per day. This is at least as much time as you would spend managing the personnel in an IT department in your company. And, yes, there will be some days where you won't deal with the MSP at all, and some days you will be very busy with them. This is just an estimate. But you must make time for it.

Hiring an MSP does not let you off the hook for managing your information systems. If you are not budgeting the time to look at reports, to follow up with your employees who are experiencing computer issues, and to touch base with your MSP account manager, you may be doing a great disservice to your company. Frequently, employees will wait for a technician from the MSP to show up at the office before they divulge their problems or questions. This should be curtailed by encouraging your people to contact the MSP via phone or e-mail prior to these visits. Perhaps you could have a monthly lottery drawing for the three people who opened up the most legitimate tickets with the MSP.

You also need to keep your ear to the ground and proactively discover ways in which your company might be able to utilize new technology. Bring these ideas up with the MSP and keep the dialog going.

A successful MSP engagement requires interactive feedback, the hallmark of good communication. One of the biggest mistakes a company can make is to assume they no longer have to deal with IT issues at all: that they can wash their hands of the responsibility. This is like saying that when you hire an accounts payable clerk that you no longer have to worry about paying bills or balancing your corporate checkbook: oversight and involvement are always necessary.

Additionally, you need to be engaged with information technology and bring the right people from your company into meetings with the MSP. All too frequently, the person in charge of managing the relationship with the MSP does not have the authority to make strategic IT decisions when the time comes to make them. Either this person can't sign off on new proposals or can't understand the implications and ramifications of new technology initiatives. Time and again, I have seen clients sit in meetings and listen to proposals, take notes directly on the presentation materials, and then leave to explain everything to the technology committee, the managing partner, or the CEO. Inevitably, the committee, the managing partner, or the CEO have a question that this person can't answer. Every time this happens, it erodes the committee's/CEO's/managing partner's confidence in the people involved in the process, including the MSP, and makes it that much harder to advance a protechnology agenda and get anything done.

What Information Will the MSP Have Access To?

Your MSP is a vendor, but there is no closer relationship your company will ever have with any other company unless you go through a merger. The MSP will have administrator-level control over your network operations. The MSP has access to all of your company's secrets: all e-mail, all files, all payroll documents, all Internet browsing history, all pictures on your network or your computers, all chats, etc.

If this is a problem for you, either you will need to accept it and move on or you will need to hire an IT person/department. No independent studies have been publicly released, but it is generally accepted that you are no more at risk of an MSP employee disclosing confidential information than you are from your own employees. According to a paper researched for computer solutions company Symantec (located at **http://www.symantec.com/about/news/release/article.jsp?prid=20111207_01**), theft of IP data most often occurs by employees who have already accepted a job at another company, and are predominantly men in technical positions (scientists, managers, engineers, and programmers).

Security and Control

To maintain an appropriate level of control, always have a copy of your corporate domain administrator password (i.e., the "god password") and local workstation administrator passwords on hand, preferably in a locked safe or file drawer. If you have a regimen of password renewal, part of that regimen should be that you get a non-electronic copy of the password(s) each time a change is made.

There are three reasons to do so:

First, this information is fundamentally crucial to the ongoing health and operation of your network, and it is your responsibility to know it or have access to it.

Second, if you are going to rebid the MSP contract or have a vendor come in to do a quality control check on your current MSP, the vendor will need this password to run any scans on your network to check for problems or to verify information from your RFP. If you do not have the domain administrative password, you will need to get it from your current provider (or employee), and it will be obvious why you are asking for it. If this is part of your schedule, you will always have a copy of the appropriate passwords, and nobody at the MSP will be any wiser. Nobody asks for the admin password unless they are going to use it, unless it is part of a predictable schedule of password changes.

Third, and finally, the regular password change regimen forces the MSP to use appropriate passwords for appropriate functions.

Regularly changing the domain administrator password discourages the MSP personnel from using it à la carte, to run backups, database administration consoles, or scheduled network tasks. Autonomy of network accounts is very important.

Computer Use Policies

If you do not have a computer use policy that your employees have read, agreed to, and signed, you should ask your MSP to help you draft one. This will go far to limit your liability should one of your employees use an office or company computer to perpetrate illegal acts. Your MSP may have a boilerplate computer use policy that can be minimally modified and implemented for your use. If you already have a policy, the MSP should have a copy on file so that they are familiar with its tenets and do not accidentally violate them in helping employees from your company.

6

The RFP—Craft Your Selection Criteria to Weed Out Unqualified MSPs

One of the biggest deciding factors in your choice to employ an MSP is the answer to the question, "How much is this going to cost?" You don't want to write an RFP that will elicit responses from MSPs proposing million-dollar solutions alongside proposals quoting $50,000 annually. This will be a waste of your time and the MSP's time. Therefore, you need to determine your annual budget for this service. But how can you figure out what your monthly or annual budget figure will be if you have never talked to an MSP before?

For starters, don't call an MSP to find out what your budget should be. At this point in your process, it can do no good and will likely introduce you to an MSP which might not be qualified to support your company, and will likely need more information from you to make a reasonable guess.

To build a budget for a service you need, but which you have never used before, can be a tricky prospect. There are a few roundabout methods you can use to get a good idea of what this is going to cost. These methods also serve the purpose of educating you and your company about IT services and the industry you are about to engage. You won't get a cookie-cutter pricing solution, but following these methods will help you think about this type of service as an expense your business needs to make in order to be competitive and prosper.

First, do some research and find out how much you have spent on technology over the past 5 years. This will not only show you what your IT costs have been (for backups, core network equipment and desktops, cables, printers, computer repair [service/consulting], Internet connections, e-mail and phone service, etc.), but will help you to spot any trends that might be emerging. Are your IT costs going down? Up? These costs will probably continue the trend you see over the past 5 years, with periodic spikes as technology is replaced. Remember, the annual or monthly cost of the MSP will be added to the costs of your current IT expenditures. The MSP is a service provider, and you will still need to pay for everything you have been paying for up to now, with the exception of a T&M vendor.

Next, reach out to friends and professional colleagues (the same network you would use if you were looking for a job) and find out if they are using an MSP, and if they are, what they are paying, who they are using, and what services they get for the price. This will also give you the names of some MSP companies to which you can send your RFP at the end of this process.

Finally, look at the obvious alternative: In a metropolitan area, hiring a basic IT person for your office will cost a minimum of $60,000 annually in salary, and $12,000 for administrative overhead. This works out to $6,000 per month. This can be expensive for a small or midsized company. Slice and dice the above salary figure to understand the value of the MSP. The size and complexity of your organization and your line of business (LOB) applications will play a factor, but, generally speaking, the ratio between employees and computer personnel is about 60:1. That is, for every 60 employees, you will need one help desk person working 8 hours per day. Extrapolating this, if you have 30 employees (half of 60), then you only need half of a computer person per day, or a full computer person for 4 hours per day. So cut the cost in half of your "phantom" IT support person in the earlier example, and you get $3,000 per month. This is a vast oversimplification, but now you have a few ways of thinking about how to come up with a reasonable price for the services you want.

It is not uncommon for a "high-touch" client of 50 people to pay upward of $12,000 per month for MSP services. It all depends on your company's needs, which you will develop as you build your RFP. Generally speaking, your company will pay more to get more personalized attention. If you want the MSP to send someone to your office several times per week, the cost will be higher than if you merely need a biweekly or monthly visit.

Now that you have a good idea as to what your IT expenses have been up to the present, and you have a framework for comparing the potential costs of hiring an MSP vs. hiring an employee, you can start to compile the data for use in your RFP. See Appendix A for a simple guide to finding and hiring an MSP. Appendix B contains a sample RFP.

The data you will need for your RFP consists of a rundown of your current IT situation. Some MSPs will ask to audit your network prior to responding to an RFP because some RFPs do not contain the information the MSP needs to make an informed proposal. If you do this for your RFP, the MSP will be able to respond more quickly with a more accurate proposal.

Also, state in the RFP if you currently are using an IT service provider, and whether your company has any upcoming projects. Usually companies begin looking for IT help when they start to grow quickly, when they lose key personnel, or they have an upcoming project. In any case, you should state the underlying cause in the RFP. If it is project related, be sure to mention the upcoming project in the RFP, and whether the MSP will be involved.

7

Don't get "$OLD!"

An MSP leverages their experienced information systems profession-
als, backed by good processes, automation and technology, to make
money.

Some mistakes I've known MSPs to make on the sales side are
breathtaking. Here are some examples:

- Presenting a solution to a client which the MSP had not
  yet implemented, even in a lab environment.

- Selling services without any input from the MSP's project
  management, on-boarding, or operations teams. An MSP
  sold full IT management services to an association. After
  the sale, the reality of what had been agreed to became
  apparent to the management of the MSP. The MSP had no-
  where near the resources to execute what the sales team
  had promised. This led to an epic disaster. The MSP threw
  so many resources at this client that every other customer suffered and the project was beset by implementation
  problems.

- Selling MSP solutions as if they were copiers. The salesperson was not prepared for the lengthy back-and-forth
  from the client. The client was trying to accomplish an
  infrastructure upgrade, which is fairly complex even without the added stress of high-pressure sales tactics. The

salesperson not only further confused the client, but he called into question the professionalism of the MSP as a whole.

These cautionary notes and examples show that not all MSPs can handle your requirements, and salespeople are not infallible or all-powerful. They are not necessarily in tune with your company's needs or with their own company's capabilities and resources. If an MSP is taking on a new client, they should have the infrastructure to be able to absorb the new work or should be planning to staff-up to address it. Size does matter. The ratio of 60:1 is typically accepted as standard to show the number of employees to computer support personnel in an organization. This goes for MSPs as well (for a customer base of 1,000 people, the MSP should employ approximately 16 help desk people). Additionally, any service over and above help desk services will require additional resources, and those need to be budgeted for, as well at the MSP.

You need to audit and understand the detailed qualifications of potential MSPs. This due diligence should be part of the RFP process. There are questions you can ask that will help you gauge the MSP's "readiness" for action. Some of these questions can be included in your RFP, but some will have to wait until you have a salesperson from the MSP in your office. Chief among your concerns is that the MSP has the infrastructure and staff to support your current needs. Salespeople will be glad to share information about the certifications their employees have, or give you hand-picked references, but they might balk at other questions which may give you a better idea about whether they can handle your company's needs. Some questions to ask include:

Question 1: How big is your company (total employees and approximate gross revenue)?

Question 2: How many employees do you have (list them by job function)?

Question 3: How many full-service clients do you have, and approximately how many of your staff work at them?

Question 4: Can I talk to a help desk person/support/engineer/project manager at your company?

These questions, especially Question 1, sound invasive, but remember that the MSP you eventually hire will have access to the most intimate details of your company's operations, including access to any financial documents you have on your network.

Do not make your decision to hire an MSP based on how well you get along with the salesperson.

Never make a decision to sign a contract in front of a salesperson or for a salesperson. Making this decision personal will ruin all of your efforts up till now to select the most qualified vendor. Sign the contract when you are convinced it is the right thing for your business. It goes without saying that you are doing your best to get the right vendor for your company. Salespeople are frequently the conduits through which these services are sold, and once you have made your decision to sign with an MSP, you should feel comfortable building a good relationship with the salesperson. After all, salespeople can usually get things done quickly in any organization because they are part of the revenue stream, and having a good salesperson on the inside can make all the difference between a good experience and a great experience.

MSP Pricing Models

MSP service price offerings vary because there are different ways to structure their service offerings. This can make comparing any two MSP solutions difficult at best. The conventional wisdom about pricing changes almost weekly with the advent of new technology, marketing initiatives, and increased competition.

One pricing model essentially compares all the money you, the client, can save by using a flat-rate model versus hiring employees to do the job. Sometimes this is called "value pricing." Everything is included: RMM, help desk, site support, advisory (CIO) services, etc. The "Per User" or "Per Device" model is simple math: count how many employees or hardware devices need to be covered, and that gives you the monthly price (I like this for its honesty and simplicity). The "Tiered" services model allows the MSP to offer different types and levels of service (including SLAs) per price point ($1,000, $1,500, $2,000, etc.). The "Pick" pricing model defines certain types and levels of service (like in the "Tiered" model) from which you can choose. The "À La Carte" pricing model splits all of the services out and allows the customer to pick exactly what they want (usually with a minimum commitment level). Finally, there is the basic "Monitoring Only" option. This is probably what a customer who has an internal IT staff would choose. Critical alerts will notify the MSP when there is a problem, and the MSP will notify your on-site contact. Your staff can then choose whether to let the MSP handle the issue or to handle it themselves.

Summary:

Don't select an MSP in front of the salesperson, and meet with at least three MSPs to get a good sampling of the market. You wouldn't only visit one dealership if you were buying a car or get only one opinion if you were diagnosed with a terrible disease, so don't hold back. This decision will have far-reaching effects.

8

Monitoring and Reporting

Good information is the foundation of strategic planning. Good reporting is necessary for good information, and good monitoring is necessary for good reporting. They all tie in together.

In the RFP, ask for submittals to be accompanied by a sample report. Be sure you understand the reports provided. An easy-to-understand report is essential to communicate effectively with the MSP and with internal company stakeholders. If an MSP does not have a good reporting package, think seriously before engaging them. If they cannot provide good information to you, either they are not collecting it or they have a systemic issue and can't regurgitate it. In either case, you don't want to be involved with them.

Accurate reporting allows you and the MSP to make operational and strategic decisions about your IT infrastructure based on empirical evidence. Without reporting, you may as well guess what needs your attention. MSPs should be able to run reports to give you the following information:

Report Metric	Operational Meaning	Strategic Impact
Total # of Machines	Old machines being reported indicates sloppy cleanup, and too few machines means they have not been added to the monitoring set.	If company size is changing, resources need to be reexamined.
Summary of Antivirus Status	Machines may not be connected to the network, or another problem.	Can be indicative other means of protection are necessary.
Summary of OS Installations	Indicative of hardware age. Is it still supported? Patched?	Software upgrade needs.
Summary of Security Patches	Maintenance may be necessary. Patches protect computers.	Can be indicative of the need for a procedural modification.
Warranty Status of Hardware	Hardware should never be out of warranty. Renew warranty or replace machines with ones under warranty.	Look ahead and plan next system upgrade.
Server Utilization Summary	Space, CPU, memory, page file, and uptime statistics. Exceeding thresholds can indicate operational issues.	Are additional resources needed? Can it wait for a systemwide upgrade?
Service Request Summary	Are service requests being generated and completed?	Service requests can show trends and needs.
Backup Reports	Indicates whether this key aspect of disaster recovery is working. Data backup is basic and critical.	Backup reports show trends in data usage. When will the backup system need to be replaced at current growth rates?
ISP Bandwidth Utilization	Are people recreationally surfing the web or streaming music and video? Is there adequate bandwidth for business operations?	Good when renegotiating telecom contracts and planning upgrades.
Project and Research Issues	This is a summary of any projects or research being undertaken by the MSP.	Project delays and researching can affect other projects.
Firewall Activity	Can indicate security issues. Attacks can impact performance of your Internet service.	Are countermeasures necessary? Should penetration testing be scheduled?
Spam Activity	Spam can impact productivity. How is your system at catching and quarantining spam?	Stronger spam filtering may be necessary to further cut spam.

Reporting is by no means useful only to your company. The MSP needs to pay attention to these reports as well. It is how they maintain and improve their services to you. If you are growing month after month, in a year you could add 12 people. This wouldn't necessarily be noticed by the MSP unless they not only had good reporting, but also had someone in their office (i.e., your account manager) reading and understanding the reports.

Finally, no less than on an annual basis, ask for a report containing the current list of your MSP's partnerships, employees' certifications, and current references. Personnel come and go at MSP companies, and so will their certifications. Likewise, an MSP who is a Microsoft Gold partner one year might not opt for the same level in the following years. This can be important to you and your auditors. Changes can suggest many things: changing business alliances or a booming or busting business. If you want a new backup system and you know the MSP has a partnership with Symantec, you might understand why their primary backup recommendation to you is a Symantec product.

9

Purchasing Goods and Services from Your MSP

It isn't a bad idea to use your MSP to purchase hardware, software, and services. But the potential conflict of interest in purchasing goods and services from the same vendor who is recommending them should not be ignored.

Many MSPs have specialties, but in today's competitive marketplace, they are all trying to be your "One-Stop Shop" to increase their revenue. This has good and bad implications. On one hand, all of your technology needs can be addressed by one vendor, negating the need to maintain relationships with multiple vendors and coordinating them. On the other hand, be aware of the old proverbial admonition against putting all your eggs in one basket, and tread thoughtfully.

Let's look at a hypothetical scenario involving purchasing goods from an MSP:

You need to replace three computers in your organization. It is much easier to order them from the MSP than to get separate quotes from different vendors, and then coordinate the shipping and receiving with your MSP so they can set them up. Like most value-added resellers (VARs), MSPs typically add a 30 percent surcharge to hardware and software orders, above what you would pay if you bought directly from the manufacturer (as in the case with Dell) or distributors like CDW or Ingram Micro. If you are ordering three PCs, the price could be $3,000 plus this 30 percent surcharge, for a total of $3,300. The 30 percent they are charging you on the hardware goes to cover the administrative fees of coordinating all of that.

On big-ticket items, this covers more than just the administrative fee for ordering the product: you are paying for the expertise for finding the right product, ordering, and coordinating the receipt of the product, and the project management for ensuring a technician is available to set up the product. If you are ordering 30 PCs, the price could be $30,000 plus 30 percent surcharge, for a total of $33,000. The same amount of work goes into ordering the same item multiple times, so you would be within the bounds of fairness to ask for a discount on larger orders. However, if the order is full of a bunch of single-item products (a firewall, a switch, a server, a SAN, etc.), the price could also be $30,000, plus the 30 percent surcharge. It takes time to research and compare and find the best products for a solution, and in these cases, consider yourself fortunate that your MSP has the expertise to make these decisions, and do not begrudge them the relatively slim profit margins they are working with. Don't ask for a discount in this case.

Now let's look at a hypothetical scenario involving purchasing services from an MSP:

If you decide to make the business decision to order a service solution like hosted (remote) backup, hosted e-mail, hosted Share-Point, etc., from your MSP, you are potentially handing the MSP a huge revenue stream. It looks good to you because you can pay the MSP a flat fee (usually monthly) for performing this service, and you will never have to worry about paying for hardware or software ever again. Your payment will remain fixed, relative to a simple formula of space used or accounts utilized. (Obviously, the more resources you use, the more you will pay: but the formula is laid out clearly so there are no surprises to you.)

Selling hosted services is attractive to an MSP because their costs for providing the service go down while yours stay contractually the same. Costs for bandwidth, storage, and rack space in a data centers go down over time: the $10 per mailbox you are paying on January

1st only costs the MSP about $7 per mailbox, and a year later it might only cost them $5, and a year after that, only $3. But you are still paying them $10 per mailbox. This is very similar to the model employed by telecommunications companies: they sign you up to a multiyear contract, and the first year they essentially cover their expenses for provisioning the service, the service itself, and the sales commission. However, telecommunications companies renegotiate their wholesale rates several times per year, thereby making each of the following years of a multiyear contract flush for them. By the second or third year, you might be paying more than 100 percent what they pay for the bandwidth wholesale.

If possible, negotiate new rates regularly and avoid lengthy multiyear fixed-price contracts. Again, MSPs should be able to profit from the services they are selling (this is why they do what they do), but there is a fine line between fair profit and price gouging, and you owe it to yourself and your company to get the best price available.

10

MSP Projects

You will likely rely upon your MSP to plan and execute projects during your relationship. A project is a service provided by the MSP, and as such, will generally require a separate scope of work. Some projects will be small and not have much impact, other than to replace this network device or that computer, or install new software. A larger project may require the MSP to engage many of their employees across different skill sets, and last several months.

Flat-fee projects encourage the project manager and the MSP to finish the project as quickly as possible, because the financial burden is on them: if they estimate the project will take 2 weeks, and it goes longer, the cost comes out of the MSP's profits and can possibly eat into their actual costs. You may think that the MSP should eat the cost, but all that does is punish the MSP for not digging deeply enough in the planning phase of the project. The sad truth about project management is that planning and discovery are ongoing through the project life cycle, and the chance always exists that something will be uncovered which wasn't taken into account in the initial assessment. If this can be absorbed into the project schedule, all is good. However, sometimes the discovery requires the project to be substantially recalibrated. When this happens, the project manager will engage all of the stakeholders to bring the new information to the table for a discussion about how this will affect the project. In this case, the cost of the project should be adjusted.

If you fight this adjustment, the next time they run a project for you, they may overestimate the time it will take to avoid a similar situation. Subsequently, you will end up paying far more in the long run over the course of many projects than you would have if you and the MSP could have negotiated a simple change order with a "no harm/ no foul" understanding.

The alternative to the flat-fee project is the hourly billed project. This is probably not the best way to set up a project, but it can be effective in an open-ended engagement (where the scope of the project may heavily depend upon factors not under the MSP's control, such as when the MSP must coordinate with other vendors or in researching a problem or an issue). Projects billed hourly should always have a set-cost point whereby the MSP will stop working (and billing) upon further instructions/approval of time from you.

11

All Eggs in One Basket?

As previously mentioned, many MSPs offer free services like e-mail hosting, corporate antivirus, and spam filtering in order to sweeten the pot and make their proposal more attractive to you. Any one of these services can cost thousands of dollars per year if you buy them from different vendors, and it can be tempting to be swayed by these freebies.

The MSP does this because it is easier and cheaper for them to support your company if you are using a standard and centralized (or centrally managed) system which services all their clients. These freebies cost them next to nothing after factoring in the labor they save over the long term from cleaning viruses or managing your e-mail servers and antispam services. Not to mention, it helps them get your business.

This is all well and good, but ask questions. If your MSP is hosting your e-mail for free, find out how much it would charge you to host your e-mail if you were to switch MSPs down the road. Get the answer in writing, because it is likely at some point that you will need or want to switch providers. Additionally, if the MSP decides to stop providing a service they previously provided gratis, how does this impact you? What is included in transitioning your mail to another provider or in getting a new corporate antivirus package rolled out to your systems? Who will pay for that? It will involve a major disruption to your business, and if this is going to happen on their schedule, not yours, be prepared, because this kind of transition usually requires downtime. There is no such thing as asking too many questions.

Be wary of a vendor who stops you and makes the blanket statement, "We've got it covered." Find out how they have it covered.

On top of this, the MSP wants to be your advisor, your hardware and software vendor, your project manager, your integrator, and your help desk. It is understandable that the MSP wants to fully monetize their relationship with you by being your single technology vendor. The good thing about this kind of relationship is that your vendor is always paying attention to the needs of your company, because you are always in the process of buying something from them. This gives you a lot of leverage. The bad news about putting all your eggs in one basket is that you will only see and be exposed to the technology solutions that they want you to see. There may be cheaper, better deals on e-mail hosting platforms, or backup solutions, but you won't know about them because your MSP is filtering all of these alternative solutions out. This could cost you thousands of dollars per year.

It comes down to trust and best practices. In truth, there are hundreds of backup solutions on the market today. You don't really need to see them all. You need to trust your vendor to give you what you need, without having to do the painstaking research and analysis yourself. Keep in mind that if you had an IT employee, s/he would also have to make the same culling decisions. It is reasonable to discuss your needs, and then to rely on the vendor to come back with three or four alternatives, which you can discuss and choose from.

Technology is constantly in flux, and the MSP not only has to stay on top of the trends and anticipate your needs and questions, but also to make active recommendations for your business when the time is right. Conversations with your MSP about technology trends should occur frequently, not just when they have something to sell you or when it is time for a technology upgrade.

If you are somewhat worried about the solutions brought to you by your MSP, either because you don't understand technology well enough to be able to properly evaluate them or because you feel the solutions are biased toward solutions which enrich the MSP, you may want to consider hiring a separate strategic IT consultant. This is someone who can help you properly evaluate solutions and make strategic and operational decisions.

12

MSP Limitations

The MSP is as familiar with your company as you allow them to be. The more they know about your company, your business, the better they will be at helping you to achieve your business goals.

MSPs can have staffing and resource limitations. They may have an inappropriate person answering their phones. They may be trying to hire new personnel to address shortcomings. However, the preponderance of MSP limitations will be perceptive rather than actual: that is, it is more likely that you will perceive a limitation or a flaw in the MSP than there actually being a real shortcoming. As Lee Atwater famously said, with a bit of brevity in paraphrasing Niccolò Machiavelli, "Perception is reality."

Much of this comes back to the initial RFP: you may be expecting a service for which you did not sign up. Or perhaps the MSP oversold you on their capabilities; or you expected more comprehensive (or less comprehensive) interaction with MSP personnel. This further reinforces why you need to have a thorough RFP, and you need to read and understand all the proposals that come as a response to it.

If you think your current MSP is lousy and you are unhappy with them, they might just as easily see you as a terrible client with unreasonable demands and impossible expectations. Perhaps you feel as if they no longer value you as a client. Perhaps they feel that you are not taking their recommendations seriously. "Attitudes" go both ways, and if you think changing your MSP is going to fix the problem, you could be wrong. All relationships involve communication: and communication goes both ways. Before switching your MSP, meet with them first to try to find common ground. Repair the communication issues. Sometimes these relationships need a reboot, just like a computer.

By and large, interactive communication will ensure minimal problems. If you and your account manager at the MSP are not communicating well, there is a good chance that you will perceive the MSP as having more limitations and shortcomings. Perhaps you have been busy and have not had a chance to sit down and talk with your account manager in a while; or perhaps your account manager has been unusually busy to adequately follow up with you. No matter: The remedy is the same. Pick up the phone and give them a call. Don't send an e-mail: Call your account manager and set up a meeting. Tell them what's bothering you. It is likely that they aren't aware of your concerns and will be surprised. A good conversation can go a long way toward getting back to good.

You should be spending some time each day (on average) managing the MSP. You can't hire an employee without taking the time to manage him or her: an MSP is essentially a contract employee. There is no way around the fact that they need to be managed. If you are not in some way dealing with your MSP regularly, it could lead to problems.

There are times when a business decision forces your company to implement a solution that your MSP cannot, for whatever reason, initiate, manage, or support. Perhaps you have the need to hire a developer to create an internal application, or perhaps you need to implement an application that your MSP has no experience with. Regardless of the situation, the MSP should be involved, even passively, from the outset. Most MSPs work well with subcontractors, and adding a new "thing" should not, in and of itself, be a deal breaker.

If your MSP is unable to support your new project for whatever reason, you should have a candid discussion about whether you should continue to contract with them. If you are in a business vertical market, like law, health care, or finance, and your company has made the decision to pursue a specialty vertical market application, like a document management system, or a medical inventory control system, or a point-of-sale system, you might want to investigate MSPs already working in that arena for continued support.

Finally, other resource limitations can come into play as well. For example, if your personnel expect to be able to call the MSP help desk for assistance with applications like Word or Excel or Outlook, and they find that the help has become less helpful over time, perhaps the MSP is not keeping their help desk staffed by people familiar with those applications. This is a legitimate complaint, and the MSP should be told about it so they can either get the proper training for their staff or hire the appropriate staff to support your company.

13

The Dream Scenario—A Strategic and Operational Balance

Call me old-fashioned or self-serving, but outsourcing all of your IT roles leaves a lot to be desired. Operationally, there is a lot to be saved and gained by doing so. But outsourcing the managerial or strategic aspects invites an inevitable conflict of interest. It would be like outsourcing your COO, CFO, or managing partner: it saves a lot of money, but nothing beats the loyalty of an employee or dedicated consultant. Ideally, the person responsible for strategic IT planning and network operations oversight at your company works for your company. They know what your finances look like; they know the bottom line. This is someone who would hold the title CIO, vice president, or director of information technology.

Smaller companies rarely have the resources for this kind of staffing, so it is a nonissue for them. The IT responsibility usually falls to the person responsible for general administration and operations. In this case, these companies would do well to require a nontechnical person in this role to beef up his or her technical understanding by taking some classes and attending seminars on topical technical subjects. There is a basic level of technical understanding needed to be able to make good IT decisions.

From an operational standpoint, it makes sense to have a desktop support person on-site to assist with operational computer issues as they come up. I think most businesses of 40 or more people can afford this. In fact, I would argue that most businesses of this size cannot afford NOT to fill this type of position. And when the strategic and the operational positions are filled with competent employees, the vast middle can be filled with an MSP presence that can act as a backup, a stopgap, an intellectual and experiential resource, and a monitoring and reporting bulwark. They can also deal with primary emergencies after-hours before involving employees.

Dream Scenario— A Strategic and Operational Balance

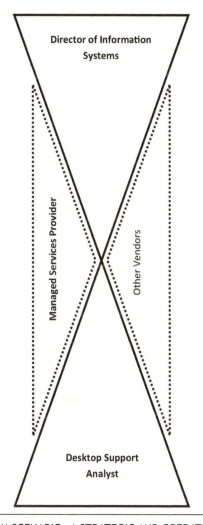

Appendix A: How to Hire an MSP: the Basics

1. Write down your reasons for hiring an MSP; this will make up the narrative of your RFP.
2. Calculate your budget for this service; this should go in the RFP as well. Note in the RFP that the budget number is an estimate.
3. Write down your answers to the following questions:
   a. How big is your company, what business are you in, and where are you located?
   b. Number of servers and the operating systems and applications on them
   c. Number of computers and the operating systems and applications on them
   d. Type of backup system
   e. Type of e-mail system
   f. Type of antivirus system
   g. Types and quantity of mobile devices (iPads, iPhones, BlackBerry, droids, etc.)
   h. Types of services you are interested in:

     i.   Advisory or CIO services

     ii.   Remote management and monitoring (RMM)

    iii.   Break-fix

    iv.   Help desk (usually part of the RMM above)

     v.   Site visits (wellness visits)

i. Identify any special compliance requirements you need to meet, like HIPAA (and HITECH), SAS 70 Type II, FINRA, SOX, PCI-DSS, etc.

j. Identify any special upcoming IT projects you foresee, or other non-IT-related projects (frequently non-IT-related projects become IT-related projects).

k. What is your deadline for selecting an MSP? When do you want to go "live"?

l. Will you expect the MSP to make house calls for staff? How many staff?

4. Prepare your RFP using the information from 1, 2, and 3. See the RFP template provided in Appendix B.

5. If you are currently using an MSP and are looking to rebid your business, do not meet with new MSPs "just to see what's available." This is a good approach to job seeking, but a decent MSP salesperson can influence you to bypass legitimate due diligence and throw your lot in with them. Do not make a decision to engage an MSP without multiple quotes and without meeting at least three of them. Ideally, an MSP which is a good fit for your organization can be a partner, can grow with you, and won't rush you through the process. If you feel pressure, it is not a good fit.

6. Send the RFP to a large sampling of MSPs in your area. (Do an Internet search for "Your City, managed services provider," and you will get plenty of hits. Also, ask around at professional organizations you belong to and scan your industry periodicals in order to find MSPs working in your market and your company niche.)

7. If you have prepared your RFP with enough attention to detail, the only responses you will get will be from MSPs who can service your company's needs.

8. When meeting with respondents, focus on the positive. Focus on your RFP; don't engage in a conversation about how lousy your current situation is.

9. Expect more work. Hiring an MSP will take up more of your time and require more of your attention than you think it will. If you are not dealing with IT issues or with the MSP between 5–15 percent of each day, something is wrong. Read the reports. Talk to your account manager. Talk to the people in your company using the services of the MSP.

10. Always have an exit strategy, always have your administrator credentials, and always dedicate yourself to making sure the MSP succeeds. If the MSP succeeds, you succeed—and your company succeeds.

Appendix B: Sample RFP for Soliciting Bids for Managed Services

This sample cover sheet is followed by a sample RFP. You will need to make substantial changes to it in order to allow it to fully represent your company to a potential solution provider.

My Company Name
123 Road; Suite 1
Washington, D.C. 11111
202-555-5555
www.mycompanyname.com

Confidential Request for Proposal for
Full-Service IT Management

Responses Due by COB 1/1/2015

Introduction:

MyCompanyName ("The Company") is the premier manufacturer and installer of low-melting point utility access covers for waste systems in Washington, D.C. The Company was formed in 1896 and provides utility access covers to local municipalities. The Company employs 92 computer users, many of whom have access to The Company's e-mail system from mobile devices (enumerated below). The nature of The Company's business requires some employees to have remote access to the network.

The Company invites all qualified third-party technology support vendors to submit proposals for full-service IT management, encompassing the description of services required in the following section.

The Company operates a hybrid Linux/Microsoft Windows networking environment. The core network consists of eight (8) servers (both physical and virtual) and three (3) utility computers that run legacy applications on Windows XP. There are approximately 95 workstations running Microsoft Windows 7 SP1 and Office 2013. There are 22 networked printers, and five (5) networked copier/printer/scanner/fax multiuse devices, for which separate maintenance contracts exist. This RFP excludes the maintenance of the printers and copiers, except where the equipment interfaces with the network and the employees via cabling, print servers, and network scanning applications. The Company's IT environment and primary applications are:

- 5 Windows Servers 2008 R2
- 2 Windows Servers 2003
- 1 Linux server (Dell Ubuntu)
- Cisco ASA 5510 Firewall
- Comcast Business Internet 20Mb down/5Mb up—no backup line
- Symantec Backup Exec to tape backup
- Iron Mountain Tape Archive Service—weekly tape rotation
- Microsoft Exchange 2010
- BlackBerry Enterprise Server 4.1
- 95 Dell OptiPlex 9110 computers running Windows 7 SP1

- Microsoft Office 2010, Service Pack 1
- Adobe Acrobat Pro XI
- Intuit QuickBooks for AP/AR
- ADP payroll
- GoToMyPC for remote workstation access (on 20 computers)
- Norton Antivirus on servers and workstations

Description of Services Required:

Hardware Monitoring and Maintenance

- Monitor servers and essential networking equipment (including UPSs, firewalls, Internet connection, switches, server room temperature and humidity) 24/7
- If monitoring parameters are exceeded or services are interrupted, execute established response procedures within SLA time frame
- Maintain all servers, firewalls, switches, cabling, battery backup systems, workstations
- Liaise with hardware support providers
- Manage, monitor, and report on the firm's data backup system
- Document all system upgrades, fixes for common problems, new configurations, implementations, etc.
- Ensure all systems are available 24/7/365, except for scheduled maintenance

Software Monitoring and Maintenance

- Monitor and maintain all server-based core company software applications, including troubleshooting, virus cleanups, installing upgrades, and integration
- Create and maintain workstation images
- Maintain print server and printing system for all networked printers and copiers
- Liaise with software support providers

- Ensure all systems are available 24/7/365, except for scheduled maintenance

Company Support
- Provide help desk services (U.S.-based preferred)
- Provide ticketing system with tracking and reporting features
- Provide 24/7/365 emergency response
- Provide recommended scheduled network maintenance outside of business hours
- Monthly executive report on network health

Advisory and Consulting Services (CIO Services)
- Advise proactively on technology trends and best practices
- Advise and participate in software technical review and implementation
- Provide specifications for all hardware and software purchases
- Assist in drafting The Company's annual IT budget
- Professionally manage IT projects to completion with own staff or subcontractor staff within approved budget. It is understood that IT projects fall outside of the monthly services fee, and that additional fees and hardware and software costs will be applicable

Project-Related Services:

The Company anticipates an upcoming systemwide upgrade by the end of the year, and the vendor chosen will be responsible for this project. We would like to consider moving some or all of our mission-critical operations off-site to a data center. We would also like to consider virtual desktops and more robust remote access options.

Budget:

The monthly budget for the required services is approximately $4,000, not including hardware, software, and special projects.

Proposals must reflect the proposed monthly fees for the services provided, an approximate fee structure for any additional services the vendor offers which could be utilized by The Company, and a list of individual or categorical consultants' fees for its employees. Consideration **will** be given to proposals which beat or exceed the monthly budget presented herein; the monthly budget is our best approximation of what we believe the service will cost, but we realize there will be variation among vendors and included services.

Review and Selection Process:

Proposals presented in response to this RFP will be reviewed by a selection committee. Selection criteria include, but may not be limited to: competitive service level agreement (SLA), price/value of services provided, level of hardware and software expertise as indicated by vendor's industry experience, positive references from companies in a similar line of business, and the capability of the vendor to perform projects and provide consulting services.

Confidentiality/Security:

Due to the confidential nature of The Company's data, security is a primary concern. Vendors with access to The Company's systems will be required to sign confidentiality and nondisclosure agreements designed to protect against disclosure of The Company's business and client information and will be required to sign and affirm a business associate's HIPAA (HITECH) security document.

Reservation of Rights:

This RFP does not commit The Company to award a contract for services or hardware, or to pay any cost incurred in the preparation of submissions. The Company reserves the right to waive or modify any particular requirements in this RFP with or without notice and with or without cause, to accept any submissions, to reject any and all submissions, and to request new submissions.

Regulatory Requirements:

The Company is SAS 70 Type II compliant and falls under both HIPAA and HITECH statutory compliance regulations. The successful bidder will be familiar with these regulations and how they apply to technology solutions, though the responsibility for compliance remains with The Company.

Submission Requirements:

Signed proposals must be received no later than January 1, 2015. Each vendor must submit its response via e-mail, fax, or terrestrial mail to:

Jane Doe
MyCompanyName
123 Road; Suite 1
Washington, D.C. 11111
P: 202-555-5555
F: 202-555-5556
jdoe@companyname.com

The above listed officer is also your contact for any questions about this RFP. This is not a solicitation for sales or marketing calls, and the contact information listed above shall not be used for any other purpose than responding to this RFP or requesting additional information to respond to it.

Submission Format:

- **Executive Summary**
  Begin the proposal with an executive summary and discuss why you feel your company is the best qualified to provide the required services.

- **Company Profile**

Include a brief history of your company including the background and experience of key personnel within the company, number of years in business, and industries currently served. Please include a current list of valid certifications held by employees at your company (it is not necessary to break down the certifications per employee) and a list of your company's partners (for example, Microsoft, VMWare, Google, etc.).

- **Solution Specifics**
  Include detailed information about assumptions, methodology, timetables, pricing, and any restrictions. Itemize solutions and pricing as much as possible. Also, please provide a sample executive report on network health of the type that your company provides regularly to its clients.

- **Reference List**
  Please provide three (3) references from other, active customers. References from companies of a similar size in a similar industry are desirable but not necessary.

Appendix C: Glossary

Agents: A software program (or set of programs) that runs on your computer systems. They report real-time health and diagnostic information to a central monitoring server to let the MSP know the status of the system. Depending on the agents installed, they can do everything from installing security updates on your systems, cleaning out the temporary files and trash, providing remote control service for the MSP when troubleshooting a problem, and reboot your systems. Agents allow the MSP to keep an eye on your network 24/7.

BCA: Business critical application. Nowadays, almost every application is a business critical application. However, this should be defined as a core application for your business, such as e-mail or the primary software used to run your business. Typically, accounting applications fall under this auspice.

BYOD: Bring your own device. A corporate policy allowing employees to use their personal smartphones, tablets, and computers to receive and synchronize corporate e-mail, tasks, calendar, contacts, and files. There are significant security risks associated with this policy, and it should not be implemented without proper deliberation. (See also SYOD.)

Central Office (CO): A building containing telecommunications or Internet equipment which services businesses or residences.

Cloud: The Internet; the central office; the data center. Anything related to communications outside the four walls of your business in "public" space. A private cloud is a slight misnomer, but usually means either a virtual infrastructure hosted on your premises, or a segregated/dedicated area in a data center containing only your equipment and/or services.

Credentials: Usernames and passwords. Passwords for your network, computers, routers, firewalls, etc. To effectively manage your network, the MSP will require administrative access to all software and hardware. This means either they will need to know all of your administrative passwords, or they will need their own administrator-level accounts. MSPs handle credentialing differently; some will request your admin passwords and will manage your network with them. Others may require their own administrative accounts on your network and on the local machines. Either way is normal and customary.

Data Center: Typically a large, highly secured warehouse-type building containing hundreds of racks of servers, switches, routers, and other data-centric equipment. Redundant power connections, generator backups, and multiple high-speed Internet connections are standard.

Emergencies: Critical, work-stopping events. It may be that your e-mail doesn't work, your files are inaccessible, or your Internet is down.

Emergency Contact: The person or group at your company first notified by the MSP in an emergency. If there is a power outage or a critical issue with your network, the MSP will need to contact someone in your company. This person would have to be able to be contacted outside of normal business hours on their personal e-mail or phone.

EUC: End-user computing. Of or relating to a person's use of, or experience with, a computer or application.

FINRA: Financial Industry Regulatory Authority, Inc. A private body acting as a standard-setting regulator.

High-Touch: (see also, low-touch): A physical IT presence at the customer location. Also, the condition of being a company which needs more attention than a typical telephone/e-mail help desk can provide.

HIPAA: The Health Insurance Portability and Accountability Act. A law regulating the security of patient records and data.

HITECH: Health Information Technology for Economic and Clinical Health. A further law regulating the security of patient records and data and providing for penalties in cases of noncompliance.

IaaS: Infrastructure as a service. Subject to different definitions and interpretations. Generally, cloud-based, pay-for-resources-as-you-go, virtual machines including servers and desktops, storage, network, load-balancers, firewalls, and VLANs.

Latency (Low or High): Latency refers to how much time, usually in milliseconds, it takes for an IP packet (the standard Internet communication media) to get from its source to its destination. Low latency means that there is a quick response, and high latency means there is a very slow response. The perfect illustration of this is a TV news interview, when one of the reporters is far away. When the reporter in the studio asks a question to the remote journalist, there is a time delay: this is classic high latency caused by distance. There are many different reasons why you can have high latency, and distance is one of them (a poor connectivity medium and multiple gateways or hops are the other causes of high latency). You might have a fast Internet connection, but if you are using a Web site that is slow because of high latency issues, all your extra speed is wasted when communicating with that Web site.

Low-Touch: (see also, high-touch): The lack of a need for an on-site

IT person at the customer location. Good for businesses which have a highly computer-literate employee base or an employee who acts as a first line of help when computer problems are reported. Also, the condition of being a company which does not need a lot of computer help/attention.

Off-Boarding: The process by which an MSP relinquishes responsibility for a client's IT infrastructure. Usually involves multiple phases and system downtime.

On-Boarding: The process by which an MSP assumes responsibility for a company's IT infrastructure. Usually this involves multiple phases and system downtime.

RMM: Remote management and monitoring. Agents, SNMP tools, and other software and hardware tools which allow a company or an MSP to monitor and manage a company's IT infrastructure remotely. Usually involves a system of alerts and the ability to remote control a customer's hardware when not at their location.

PaaS: Platform as a service. Subject to different definitions and interpretations. Generally, cloud-based, pay-for-resources-as-you-go, Web servers, databases, etc. Used to develop mission-critical applications utilizing cloud-based tools.

PCI-DSS: Payment Card Industry (PCI)-Data Security Standard (DSS).

SaaS: Software as a service. Subject to different definitions and interpretations. Generally, a cloud-based application, such as e-mail, document management, and manipulation applications like Word or Excel, accounting applications, etc.

SAS 70: Service auditor's reports. A standardized way for a service organization to communicate information about its controls. There are two types of reports. A Type I report contains the auditor's opinion on (1) whether the organization fairly describes its controls, and the relevant aspects of the controls in operation as of a specific date, and (2) whether the controls were suitably designed to achieve specified control objectives. A Type II report contains everything in the Type I report, plus (3), whether the controls tested are operating with sufficient effectiveness to provide a reasonable assurance that the control objectives worked during the period specified.

SOW: Statement of work. Literally, a statement of work to be performed, usually including milestones, costs, and a payment plan.

SOX: Sarbanes-Oxley Act. A regulatory act applicable to all public companies. Mandates top management must individually certify the accuracy of financial information. Also, introduced penalties for noncompliance or violations and increased the independence of outside auditors who review the accuracy of corporate financial statements.

SYOD: Select your own device. A corporate policy allowing employees to select a smartphone, tablet, or computer to use to receive and synchronize corporate e-mail, tasks, calendar, contacts, and files. For example, if an employee wanted a smartphone to receive corporate e-mail, he or she would be able to choose the smartphone, but it would be provisioned by the company and only corporate functionality would be permissible on it. This means the employee would have two devices: his or her personal smartphone and the corporate smartphone. While inconvenient, this scenario is much more secure than allowing an employee to have this functionality on their personal device. If the employee were to leave, or if the phone were stolen, the smartphone could be wiped of all data and returned to factory settings and not risk wiping out the employee's personal data.

VAR: A value-added reseller. Any vendor who sells a good or a service to a customer containing additional guarantees, benefits, or services above that which is intrinsic to the good or service.

Tickets: Tickets are the electronic tracking device for every issue, problem, or request. The ticket is how the MSP keeps track of your issues and will be the way they track and report their SLA performance. Think of a ticket as a work request, like calling your plumber or your air-conditioning vendor.

www.ingramcontent.com/pod-product-compliance
Lightning Source LLC
Chambersburg PA
CBHW051211050326
40689CB00008B/1263

* 9 7 8 1 4 7 8 7 2 7 4 1 5 *